The Complete Randomness of Thoughts
By Leland Hoburg

Contents

Past Thoughts and Reflections

Do you ever wonder what your life would have been like if you had made other choices? If you had gone left instead of going right or stayed in school instead of working for a living? The choices of the past no longer matter; I am where I want to be. Older, wiser, better prepared for the difficulties of college life than the typical college freshman. Walking across campus every day I notice little differences between my fellow students and myself; the grey hairs in my goatee, their freer laughter, and the easy smiles. Life experiences change you for better or worse but they change you. As the semester winds down and most of the students' head home for the summer I just think about what I have yet to do before my life can move on.

Most Important seven seconds of your life.

Most people do not realize the most important seven seconds of any relationship is when you first meet that other person. It does not matter if it is a business, professional, or personal relationship, the thing is we compartmentalize people in our memory by physical appearance and we prejudge them by their appearance. What you need to do is remove that egg carton in your mind where you put the big blue and fuzzy individual in one place and the short one-eyed green person in another, quit judging them as a class instead of as individuals.

I am going to break a person down by using an analogy of an automobile and seven characteristics of an automobile.

1. New or Used. Age. How we relate to people is often by their age, whether they are older or younger than us. Are they more experienced than us? Have they some perspective different than ours based on life experiences? Do we instantly stereotype them because of their age as curmudgeonly? On the other hand, enthusiastic but not experienced? On the other hand, by having shared experiences? Age is a definer. We instantly deal with children differently than adults; we deal with the elderly differently than we do someone closer in age to us, but why? Is it programming? U.S. culture centers on youth, raising it up, recapturing it, while we push our elderly away and "lock" them away in places where we no longer have to deal with them. Age is a definer but not a restrictor. Treat all adults in the same way, with respect. Remove age from the stereotype category.

2. Make. Ethnicity. We have stereotypes about ethnicity; we have jokes about ethnicity that should never be

repeated; ethnicity is more than just saying, "I am a proud _____." It can truly define who we are in the eyes of others. Do we dress in traditional clothing? Do we have certain practices that are only done by members of our ethnic group? Do we follow the "hive" mind of our ethnic group? Do we live within a neighborhood that is only "us"? Ethnicity in a larger sense is where our ancestors came from, it can define us, but it should not. Ethnic groups are stereotyped. Lazy. Snobby. Untrustworthy. Stupid. Slow. Unclean. The Righteous. Bigoted. Romantic. The list can go on and on. When you turn a person into an icon, a symbol, you dehumanize them. They are no longer an individual, they are a class, and as a class, they can be ridiculed, hated, etc. People are individuals not groups, stereotypes of groups should not reflect upon the individual.

3. Model. Physical gender. Male or female. We have different mechanisms for relating to different genders, especially when dealing with the opposite gender. Physical attraction or repulsion. Again, when it comes to adults in a professional or business relationship we should not treat someone differently because of their apparent gender. Equality among the sexes in professional or business relationships. Again remove the stereotypes, treat people as individuals and not members of a class. There is no such thing as the "weaker" sex, just ask any woman who has born a child then ask any group of men if they would go through the same thing.

4. Color. Hair color, skin color, eye color. Similar to Make but different in a few ways, again we have jokes about people with certain hair colors that should not be

tolerated. The color of one's skin is genetics not a group classification. Ask my friend Angel Sanchez if he is Cuban or Caucasian. He is blonde haired and blue eyed and grew up in Miami's Little Havana, so what do you think his answer is? The answer is Cuban. Again color can be misleading, we see the outside flesh but have not yet even spoken to the person and are making judgments about them. Hitler and the Nazi's developed the "ideal" standard for the Aryan person all around the color of a person's skin, hair, and eyes; pretty interesting the "Aryan standard" was blonde, blue-eyed, and fair skinned. Hitler himself would not be considered "Aryan" enough to be an Aryan. Again, color is genetics not a definer of a group, individuals are what we are.

5. Engine. Simply put personality. Are they an enterprising person? Laid back? What is their apparent personality? This is a harder one to define. As anyone who has observed people and their mannerisms this characteristic comes up in conversation rather that physical appearance, and is harder to define. We often deal with people differently based on the impression we get from them. Do they seem aloof? On the other hand, anal-retentive? On the other hand, uncaring? Everyone is unique and dealing with different personalities or conflicting personality traits can be difficult. The key is listening to the individual, remove preconceptions from the equation.

6. Standard features. Education. Religious beliefs. Employment. Social Economic status. Regional. Again, another hard one to determine without starting a conversation, there may be some symbols and artifacts

about the person that may relate to this area but again not always apparent at first. How we interpret, what we see can define how we relate to another person. A great test is to go into any jewelry store dressed in a suit (or the equivalent) and watch the actions of the salesperson, then visit again a few days later dressed casually and notice the difference.

7. Optional features. Body type and Sexuality. Again another hard one to sometimes determine without starting a conversation. Is it any wonder that gay and lesbian teenagers have a suicide rate four times that of their heterosexual peers? Social pressures, peer pressures, and bullying, simply put sexual identity is a stressor. We should not change how we treat others by their apparent sexual identity; it is no different from their skin tone. No classifying someone by their apparent sexual identity, individual not group. As to body type this is a physical characteristic, again the bigoted jokes come to mind about a person's build. Remove the preconceptions about height, weight, size, and shape of a person. Is it no wonder in the U.S. we have issues with body image, where skinny and buff are the ideal, where few of us will ever be the ideal, where the anxiety over not matching the ideal can lead to lifelong issues.

In the end, our eyes will betray us; our preconceptions need to be removed; the egg carton in our mind thrown away; and individual treated as such.

Random thoughts

A school district in Minnesota is under investigation for civil rights violations for not being proactive or reactive in several cases of bullying that lead to the deaths of seven students over the last two years. The case revolves around the schools "gender neutrality" policy. The seven students all committed suicide, in the information left behind all pointed to the fact they had been bullied because of their sexual orientation or perceived sexual orientation. These students had been bullied at school to the point of no other perceived recourse other than to end their suffering through their own death. Bullied to death. Schools are the one-place children should feel safe, but sadly, they are not. Until we as a nation rethink our attitude towards education, towards schools, and towards funding for education; schools will remain as they are, a gladiatorial pit which the "in crowd" torments the "the outsiders."

Why is it when budget cuts come around education and educational programs are always on the chopping block? Is it any wonder why our children are failing behind the rest of the world? The United States used to be the pinnacle of education, now we are slowly sliding down the scale. Our funding of education needs to be a priority, fund the arts as well as the sciences, and quit pouring additional monies into sports programs. Path to education reform: Institute a uniform dress code, studies have found that public schools that have a "uniform" dress code have test scores rise over time, less instances of classroom disruptions, less instances of bullying, and students report less stress about going to school. Unfortunately, make interscholastic sports a "pay to play" system, if your student wants to play a particular sport you have to foot part of the bill. This is already happening around the country in smaller school districts that are strapped to fund regular classroom activities. Increase tax levies for education, educating the next generation should be priority number one not number one-thousand. Lastly, state academies for Math and Science, and for the Arts. Some areas and states already do this but every state needs to do this. Our education system is already one where the "haves" are getting more and the "haves not" are getting less; spending needs to equalize across the system.

Is it any wonder the Amy Winehouse was found dead in her home? A documented life of drug and alcohol addiction does not usually end well. Her contribution to music will be missed and her life just another cautionary tale.

Another extremist acts out against their own government, this time in Norway. As we have seen here in the United States, the actions of homegrown terrorist, my heart goes out to those families who have suffered a loss because of an act of violence against ones government. Norway, like the United States, has an elected government, a system of laws and rights, and means for public discourse, why then do individuals feel it is necessary to target children with acts of violence to make a statement against the government? Oklahoma City, and now Oslo, Norway; most of the victims were children.

Last thoughts: Congress get your act together and compromise over budget cuts and revenue increases. If our nation goes into default, you will continue to see YOUR paycheck because you are deemed necessary but many who depend upon social services will suffer. Let us try a novel idea: Congress does not get paid until a debit agreement is reached, all utilities are shut off at the Capital building until a debit agreement is reached, and all health services and health insurance for congress ceases until a debit agreement is reached. Let congress suffer along with the citizenry if a debit agreement is not reached prior to August 2, 2011.

Just some random thoughts for the day....

Is sexting cheating? A better question is: Why would you want to send compromising pictures to someone else, who is not your partner, for the purpose of receiving similar pictures in return? In the internet, age things can be spread rather quickly.

All religions attempt to explain our existence on this rock. Why should we argue over who is right when all boil down to "live a conscientious life" and "do no harm."
Your failure to act accordingly does not create an emergency for me or prompt me to take action.

If you sign up for something read the fine print, it is there for a reason.
Living healthy is expensive; no wonder we have become a nation of overweight couch potatoes.

"Just looking" means bored and your store was a convenient place to duck into.
Looking uses your eyes and not your hands, unless you are blind (of course).
Last thought this morning: Politicians or patriots? One does what is best for their career and one does what is best for their country.

Random thoughts for June 10, 2011...

Heard a commentator on the radio talking about if older generations had been "green" we would have less problems with the environment today. His comments did remind me of days gone by and how we were "green" then...

I remember when beverages came in glass bottles and you returned those bottles for credit.

I remember when the state of Iowa started giving $.05 cents refund on glass bottles and aluminum cans. You were also charged that refund amount extra at purchase.
Doing a little research, in 1940, the average family produced about two tons of garbage per year, in 2000; the average family produced about ten tons of garbage per year.

I remember when groceries left the store in paper bags, and those bags were the basis for art projects amongst other things.
We walked or rode our bikes to school, the grocery store, to our friend's house, and not had mom drive us.

I remember our garden, which provided fresh vegetables for the summer; and the canning and pickling of said vegetables in the fall; along with homemade grape jelly from our grape arbor.

Learning to cook, pre-made and prepackaged foods were expensive and rather bland tasting. I used to think TV dinners (good ole Swansons meals in a tin tray) were an inducement for being well behaved for the sitter.

Lastly, for today, water came from the faucet or a fountain not a plastic bottle with some exotic name on it for a price.

Random thoughts for June 12th, 2011...

Reading an article today about bullying and LGBT (Lesbian, Gay, Bi-Sexual, and Transgender) teens and the social pressures of being "straight" and how it shapes their self-esteem. Unfortunately, LGBT teens have a higher suicide rate than "normal" teens. Thinking about my own life and how bullying shaped my own self-esteem issues (which still cause issues for me today) and how much harder it was for friends of mine who are LGBT. Bullying usually starts around second grade when children start to notice differences and mimic their parent's biases, from that point on the cruelty continues. The issue of bullying in our schools has gotten to the point that the President and Congress are starting to weigh in on the subject and are pushing for national legislation to address the issue.

On another note from watching people go by my workplace... please wear clothes that fit properly, if you must wear heels learn to walk in them so you do not sound like a horse clomping down the street, if you insist on wearing a t-shirt with a message make sure the message does not reflect your stupidity, and lastly if you shop at my workplace do not harangue us for being open on Sunday when you are shopping on Sunday.

A great source of irony as our Soldiers, Sailors, Airmen, and Marines fight for the freedom of others along with our own freedoms, one of the freedoms upheld this year by the Supreme Court was the 1st Amendment. The church that protest at the funerals of service personnel killed in combat or die as a result of said combat are allowed to protest at those funerals. Even though the spirit of the Amendment is being abused, the letter of the law is not; sad but true.

As Bin Laden is at the bottom of the Indian Ocean, another long sought after criminal from the breakup of Yugoslavia was caught after fifteen years on the run. He is charged with attempted genocide for the deaths of five thousand ethnic Bosnian Muslims. He will be tried in The Hague. A radio commentator was comparing his capture with the situation with Bin Laden; the difference is Bin Laden orchestrated an attack on a sovereign nation as an act of terrorism not a genocidal attack on his own countrymen as the result of civil war.

On a lighter note, listening to morning drive time radio can actually be entertaining especially when the DJ's are making social commentary. This week's commentary focused around Jerks (those obnoxious individuals that cause so much frustration) and how they seem to get the girl and the promotion. I found it entertaining and thought provoking at the same time. Do Jerks always get everything? To a point they do but usually they only make it to the point their ineptitude becomes apparent, so nice guys there is always a chance to succeed.

As my fiancé and I prepare for the birth of our child, at the age of 41 and 44 respectively, everyday is to be lived and not just tolerated. It is great to have a housecat day once in a while; you lounge around the house doing what you please with the special person in your life.

Lastly, as the NBA begins its finals, the NFL draws no closer to a labor agreement, and MLB marches along, I have two words: "COLLEGE FOOTBALL!" Go Husker nation, now in the Big Ten.

Random thoughts for July 6th, 2011...

What is wrong with this picture: 187 Teachers, Principles and other school administrators in the Atlanta, GA public school system are under investigation for manipulating standardized test results to show the school was helping the students improve as shown by the raising of test scores. Here is a symptom of a larger issue when it comes to handing out money to schools for the "increases" in test results, why would a school district need to do this? Simple answer: Our education system is floundering and needs to be overhauled in such a manner that our standards match the expectations. Think of these two facts: 1. Japan graduates more engineering students from their universities than any other nation. The United States graduates more lawyers than all the European Union combined (roughly the same population).

The NBA players association should learn a lesson from the NFL players association: A Lock out is a bad thing. Hockey has not fully recovered from its fiasco several years ago with a players strike.

College football and basketball players at Division I schools are essentially professional athletes without the pay. The sooner we all recognize this the sooner we can fix problems with the system of college recruiting. To paraphrase a D-I University President "If our universities football program did not generate so much revenue for the athletic department, we could not field athletes in "Olympic sports" like swimming, wrestling and gymnastics; but because the program does generate a high level of income the university can support non-revenue generating sports."

Kudos to the state of New York for allowing same sex couples to marry. I hear the arguments against same sex marriages and I hear a replay of the arguments against allowing Whites and non-whites to marry prior to the civil rights movement. By withholding the right to life, liberty, and the pursuit of happiness to any segment of our population is akin to saying "you are not worthy of full liberties, you are beneath our consideration." When will we learn to quit legislating what occurs between consenting adults? Celebrate the freedoms we all should get to enjoy, not just the ruling elite.

They have started replacing lab rats with politicians, there are just some things that rats will not even do.

State and US legislators should have their health care premiums raised and their services slashed just like the Republicans are doing to the endangered species known as the "Middle class."

Last thought/comment: The top 2% Americans (incomes of over 2 million a year) continued to increase their net worth by a rate of 20% over the last three years while middle class saw a loss of net worth by nearly 40%. The ultra rich get richer, everyone else loses. Welcome to the Oligarchy of the United States.

Oligarchy of America

Congress is playing a game of chicken between the Republicans and Democrats over the budget ceiling. The Republicans want to cut 1 trillion in social services over the next ten years, 100 billion a year, in primarily Education, Health services (Medicare/Medicaid) and early childhood initiatives. Cuts without additional funding sources. These cuts affect about 40% of Americans. The Democrats want to close tax loopholes that affect the wealthiest 10% and roll back Bush Era tax cuts. Revenue increases without any spending cuts. These tax increases affect about 20% of Americans, earners in the $200,000 plus category for total household income.

Unfortunately, there is a compromise, some spending cuts with some revenue increases. The down side is the spending cuts will affect more Americans, especially those on assistance programs, while the tax increases will affect the top tier of income earners.

America is becoming an Oligarchy where power is concentrated in the few, the wealthy, and where the working class will be little more than place bound serfs without basic services, access to education, and proper medical care.

Welcome to the American caste system: The untouchables (working poor and persons on welfare), working class (skilled or educated labor), Merchant class (Doctors, Lawyers, Middle Management), and The Elite (CEO's, Professional Athletes, Entertainers, High Earners). Welcome to third world America.

One Tin Soldier

"Go ahead and hate your neighbor, go ahead and kill a friend. Do it in the name of religion to justify it in the end... And one tin soldier rode away..." Coven "One Tin Soldier"
A brief study of selective religious intolerance in America:

Huzzah for the Hindu community in Houston, Texas for the opening of their new temple.

Thumbs down for community leaders in Murfreesboro, TN for blocking the building of a new Mosque. It is all right for some snake handlin', tongue speakin', Holy Roller Pentecostal mega church to expand but for any other belief to do the same spikes the ire of the religious right wing.

We must remember the first amendment, freedom of religion, freedom of speech, freedom of....

We must also remember that there have been acts of terrorism supported by the Christian beliefs, the I.R.A. in Northern Ireland, Serbian purging of Ethnic Kosavians, the Inquisition, and the list rolls on...

Lastly, those without sin may cast the first stone...

Bullying, the after effect

Sitting here watching Anderson Cooper discussing bullying on his show, the story of a fourteen year old boy who committed suicide and was still bullied after his death outside of his funeral. This issue has gotten to the point that I fear for any child who does not go along with the herd. Why do we tolerate this behavior in our schools, on our sports teams, in our youth organizations, and in our daily lives? Does common decency need to be taught in our schools? Do we need to start sensitivity training in kindergarten (we start sex ed. this early)? Is it possible that we have become as adults so wrapped up in our own problems that we no longer teach our children what is proper behavior, what is acceptable, what is decent?

Bullies are just sad pathetic people with low self esteem that make themselves feel better by harassing others to the point of cruelty. The way to frustrate a bully is not to react to them. When you are out of school and it has been twenty years or more bullies are nothing more than sad and pathetic, for the most part their ways did not get them far in life.

Reading an article the other day about bullying and LGBT (Lesbian, Gay, Bi-Sexual, and Transgender) teens and the social pressures of being "straight" and how it shapes their self-esteem. Unfortunately, LGBT teens have a higher suicide rate than "normal" teens. Thinking about my own life and how bullying shaped my own self-esteem issues (which still cause issues for me today) and how much harder it was for friends of mine who are LGBT. Bullying usually starts around second grade when children start to notice differences and mimic their parent's biases, from that point on the cruelty continues. The issue of bullying in our schools has gotten to the point that the President and Congress are starting to weigh in on the subject and are pushing for national legislation to address the issue.

Let us look at the anatomy of the bullied, for one reason or another they stand out as "different." Too tall, too short, larger build, overweight, too thin, too smart, not overly intelligent, glasses, does not run fast enough or any combination of the listed factors. Most bullying starts in second grade (for me it did) when children start to notice differences between themselves and other children. Children often reflect the biases and bigotry of their parents; this reflection is not tempered by an adult's ability to self-censor around others. Children in their bluntness about their perceptions push beyond "telling it like it is" to cruelty. Like sharks sensing blood in the water, bullies keep pouring on the torturous litany of cruel words and actions.

For me, the bullying started in second grade when I got glasses. It was okay to be the short smart fat kid but it was not okay to be the short fat kid with glasses. It did not help being in a small town-small school district in farm country Illinois. My father was a teacher but we were not from the community, our family had not worked the land for the last four generations, we were different but not in a big way just different. Bullying took many different forms, from the typical knocking the books out of the hands, the fake vomit on the desk, name calling, to physical violence and the threat of violence (this was the worst). Oddly one of my worst bullies was one of my best friends, he knew exactly which buttons to push and how far to push to them, never far enough to make me snap but close enough. The bullying continued all through school, the best year for me was my senior year of high school, by that time I could care less what my classmates thought of me. I think of my successes as a youth and realized later that they were not things anyone could take away from me; they were not fleeting moments of brilliance but the result of hard work. The after effect of years of being bullied were low self esteem issues, always feeling like everything you did was never up to everyone else's standards, feeling like an outsider all the time, never being able to truly enjoy my successes. The bullying got so bad during eighth grade I wanted to end it all, thought about but never went any farther than thoughts, realizing things would eventually get better.

Realizing life would eventually get better helped me through the rough patches of my youth along with finding ways to excel that most others had passed on. Scouting was a great way to escape the bullying and to achieve success, worked my way to Eagle Scout.
2010 was my twenty-fifth class reunion, did not attend, but it made me think of those who had bullied me and those who did not. Time has been kind to some and cruel to others, some have become "good" people by giving back through service, and others are just as pathetic as they were long ago.

The way to end bullying is to not tolerate it in our schools, in our lives, in our work environments, any place we are, to stand up as a group and celebrate our differences not to ridicule those who are different.

Parents, talk with your kids, communication is the key. Keep the lines open and talk daily with them, my parents did and it helped.

I was thinking, as I am wont to do, while doing the dishes (my dishwasher is me) about the reaction to my blog on bullying, about those who never bullied me and those who I considered my friends. This ties into health issues I had several years ago and the outpouring of compassion from unexpected sources. As I was thinking about days long gone, this individual was one of those who I hardly ever interacted with when we were in school together but she was one of the first to offer moral support for the tough time I was passing through. I never really got the chance to thank her, thank you Debbie you are truly one of those people whose outer beauty matches her inner beauty.

By my earlier blog, you would think my life as a child/youth was one torturous day after another but there were moments that stand out, many more than positive ones than negative ones. I wanted to list a few of those moments and see how many more you remember...

- Playing the maitre'd in Hello Dolly
- Running the lights for Sound of Music
- Getting caught partying out at the Old Catholic cemetery
- Taking a dive on the track at the Alexis relays
- Any day in Jim Blair's geometry class with Sue Underwood and Steve Erlandson
- Any day in Jim Blair's classroom (one of my favorite teachers)
- Any night cruising Galesburg in the camaro
- Seeing Lynn Allen for the first time at Beethoven's
- Backstage during Once Upon a Mattress
- National Jamboree
- Playing D&D with my friends (and many other games)

- Scout camp (any year)
- Last one... The Football Skit for homecoming, senior year

We seem to judge our life by our accomplishments and our failures, not by how we live but by what we do. We judge our lives in relation to what others have, keeping up with the Joneses syndrome. What for? A way to measure ourselves, to add meaning to our lives, but to what point...

Have decided to post a couple of comment from my Facebook page in response to my article...

Lee, finally got around to reading your blog on bullying - and it really struck home - the bullying was so bad for me that my mom actually went to speak to the school administrators about it. She was told there was nothing they could do about it, and that if the other kids did not like me, they would not tease me.
In the 6th grade there was one girl who punched me in the stomach EVERY DAY. I spent a lot of time home sick that year.

People warn me to watch my older son that he is going to be just like those kids at Columbine (he is a gun nut). My answer is that he knows he can tell me ANYTHING and I try to stay in touch with what is going on with him.

I can honestly say that, while he has his problems and the normal pre-teen self-absorption, he can be a very insightful, caring, helpful individual. I am very proud of both my children, and make sure to tell them all the time. The good side is that even at 12 years old Monster1 will still hug me and kiss me goodbye in front of other kids. He is not ashamed to tell me he loves me... and THAT makes me proudest of all.

From a friend:

I read your article on bullying and it struck pretty close to home. In grade school, I remember feeling absolutely worthless due to bullying. It left me with a sense of fear and doubt that was difficult to overcome. Fortunately, I was able to escape through spending time with good childhood friends like you.

It probably also contributed to who I became as a teenager, which was kind of a jackass, at times. I probably mimicked and modeled some of the abuse that was laid on me. There are certainly things that I regret doing or saying as a teen. In response, I have tried to live my life as a man by treating people with understanding and respect.

If (and probably when) I directed any of my teenage angst, venom, anger, and insecurities your way, then I am truly sorry.

You are a good writer, Lee. Keep writing.

From Stacey:

So...in a nutshell, you were bullied because your parents cared about your vision and fed you well. I so understand the whole low self esteem. Still there. After attempting suicide in the 9th grade (became super sick instead of dying) I decided God was punishing me for something and took all the bullying to the point I was stuffed in instrument cases, locked in lockers for half the school day, and more. I thought if I was their target, they would leave others alone, and my life was not worth anything anyway (was in foster care at the time). It was not much better when I went back to my family. I went to college to escape and did not make friends out of fear of becoming a target again. I have had trouble making friends my entire adult life. At least as a college teacher, I can be the quiet one and not worry...why working on PhD.

You are right they may damage us physically and emotionally, but cannot take away our accomplishments.

You can visit but never truly go back.

It has been an interesting few days visiting my hometown. A small farming community tucked along the interstate in western Illinois, nestled among cornfields, soybean fields, and hog farms. The town has progressively shrunk in population over the last twenty-five years or so since I graduated from the local high school, down around thirty percent over that time period. One thing I noticed, different from where I currently live, in a walk around town (which can be done in about thirty minutes) is all the houses have yards and space between neighbors. I found places where there had been houses from my childhood that were now empty lots, and houses vastly different from days gone by. The local bars are fewer in number and the hardware store is gone, the grocery store is back in use and the library still reminds me of a used bookstore, as things change they still retain that familiar quality. Another thing I notice which is just a process of time is how the cemetery has grown and expanded.

One of the places from my youth was an empty house we all used to think was haunted. A test of fortitude was to sneak into the empty house at night and stay awhile. Very few of us ever stayed inside more than a half an hour or so before nerves and random noises got to us. I am not sure if it was haunted but it was creepy at night. Now it is fixed up and a family lives there.

On Friday night, the high school co-op had a football game (in which we won) and like many small towns across America, the local game is as much a social event as well as a sporting event. You see who is popular by their hanger-ons and who is not, who the rising stars are and who are already there and who is the next big man on campus by their performance on the field. In a way, the event cements the communities into a unified group with many little cogs. I remember from my days on the field looking back at the stands from time to time and wonder what deals were being made and what relationships were being broken but such is life. I ran into a few friends and acquaintances at the game; had a few moments to catch up but alas, since I am now an outsider, living far away, my importance to the community is lessened. I have become a story about someone who moved, whose ways were now different, whose experiences were cautionary tales about what happens when you leave but then again some I ran into have not changed much in those long years, others still lament about lost youth, and others talk about what we are each doing now and curious about our now life.

There were benefits growing up here, you could run around town without fear of strangers, but then again everyone knew what you were doing and if you were causing trouble, your parents were notified before you got home. There were some drawbacks though, everyone knew your business even if you did not want them to but that again is small town life. I remember chafing against the realities of small town life and could not wait to leave. Now there are days I long for the simplicity but one craving for sushi reminds me otherwise. I like the anonymity that city life brings, along with the conveniences.

I remember a John Mellencamp song about a small town and it is so true in many ways. Visiting serves as a reminder of where I started, not of innocence lost or paradise found, but this is where I came from but it does not define me it adds to the story of me. It is always nice to visit. Home is where your heart, is not always where you were from or where you are now, but a state of mind and being.

More Random Thoughts ...

I took a trip recently back to Illinois to visit my parents and younger daughter, and had some interesting radio listening on the drive back to West Virginia on that Sunday morning.

Heard a discussion on the new law in Illinois on Civil Unions. Kudos to Illinois for tackling the issue of gay marriage in the right sense. The Civil Union is no different from a marriage both individuals have the same rights and protections under the law as any heterosexual couple has and by that standard, the marriage certificates in Illinois starting in 2012 will all be called Civil Union certificates. The State has separated marriage from civil union by using the language "the state has a right to grant the formation of a legal union between two consenting adults" and hands the matter of a marriage back to where it belongs, religious organizations. Marriage is a religious matter while the legal formation of a union is matter for the state, separate and different, one is for legal issues, and one is to satisfy one's religious beliefs.

Surfing again through the radio channels came across a discussion on the beginnings of the push to repeal the anti-polygamy laws in the U.S., which were created to specifically target the Mormon movement and part of the government agreement, which allowed Utah to become a state. Oddly enough the U.S. is one of the few G20 nations that have anti-polygamy laws, most countries do not specifically address it as a crime but place limits on the number of adult relationships within the family unit. Remembering what a Political Science professor had once said that the laws in the U.S. had their roots in the Puritan social beliefs and our national views were shaped by as such the religious right of center view on life in general. Work hard (nothing wrong with that), family first (nothing wrong again) and place god above all else and god's law (I do have a problem with this. Which god?) were the basic puritan tenets. Personally, I do not have a problem with polygamy or polyandry (wife with multiple husbands) as long as all parties involved are consenting adults and agree to the situation. It becomes a problem when one of the parties is neither consenting nor in agreement and is forced/coerced into the situation at hand. There is a movement called "polyamorous" which is very similar to polygamy but where two individuals have a legal marriage and the third (or extra partners) is a willing/consenting participant. The home situation is very similar to a polygamist household, shared family/household responsibilities and separate sexual relations among the adult members. This skirts the legal ramifications, meaning illegal polygamist activities, by not referencing the tertiary relationship as husband/wife but as partners, and all children of the household are taken care of and treated with equality. In some way as a nation, we need to look in the mirror and see if we like the face staring back at us. In our national discourse, we talk about freedoms but do we really want to grant them? As in the phrase "Life, liberty and the pursuit of happiness," are we willing to grant fringe groups equal rights or are we just blowing smoke?

Now with college football back in full swing it is time to take a swipe at the failed BCS championship format of D1-A schools. Here is an alternative (and please read all the way through before forming and opinion): An eleven-team playoff system. Why eleven teams? There are eleven D1-A football conferences and in this system only conference champions (as determined by each conference through championship game or round robin play) would qualify, all independent teams would not qualify no matter how good their record is (Sorry Notre Dame you need to join the Big East for all sports not for all sports but football) and which university they are. Here is how the playoff would go: First round six teams would play, eliminating three, after which there would eight teams left. Next rounds would go as follows round of eight (quarterfinals), round of four (semifinals), championship game. Ten games to be televised (imagine the dollars the NCAA would generate for this system) and would add a maximum of four games to any college teams' schedule. Rules to add/change: limit teams to eleven game seasons plus conference championship game, eliminate games between D1-A (FBS) schools and D1-AA (FCS) schools, and eliminate automatic bowl bids (set bowl eligibility at minimum of eight wins). With 33 bowl games each year, use some of the lower tier bowls as neutral sites for the first two rounds, and allow the conference runner-ups to go to the traditional bowl match ups. How would the teams be placed in the bracket? Prior to the start of the college football season a lottery would determine the placement of each conference on the championship bracket (eleven balls in a lottery machine randomly drawn one at a time then placed in one of the starting eleven spots). After all conference champions have been determined, the teams are plugged into the brackets based on their conference and play begins with one round of play each week for a total of four weeks of play. Why not expand this to sixteen teams? Simply too much controversy on who was added and who was left out, conference champions only get to play for a chance at a national title. This eliminates the controversy of power conferences (Big 10, Pac 10, Big 12, etc.) getting the spotlight versus the mid majors (MAC, Mountain West, Conference USA, etc.) best being jilted at bowl time. It is time for a true national championship game not a contrived convenience created by the BCS. As certain non-power conference schools have proved year after year they can play with anybody and beat them. You would think by now the NCAA has learned their lesson with all the revenue created by the NCAA Basketball tourney and apply that logic to football. D1-A football is the only major sport national title not determined by a playoff or sport appropriate system. It is time to get it correct NCAA, not time to create more controversy.

Words of Advice

Some words of advice from my father (the Elder Hoburg) to pass along:

- Measure twice, cut once, you will never go wrong.
- Somebody always gets caught...
- Remember you are responsible for your actions; no one can make you do something you do not want to do.
- Never spit into the wind.
- Moderation is the key.
- Success involves hard work and perspiration; it is not handed to you.
- In golf keep your head down, swing smooth, and follow through. In life keep your head up, your eyes open, and be open minded.
- Treat everyone like your mother, with respect.
- Lastly, life is more interesting than fantasy, a clean joke gets just as many laughs, and friends are the family you wish you had had.

The reason I started this blog was to have a running dialog on becoming a parent again, considering my youngest is twenty, how we went from being empty nester's to future parents. First was the realization that we were going to be parents with those mixed feelings of scared shitless and crazy happy. Of all the things we were going to go through, this is her first, from changing diapers (by the toilet, oh the smell), to potty training, to doctor and hospital visits, to all of the other million experiences you have with kids. It seems strange to be a grandparent and a future parent all at the same time. Life has afforded me another chance at being a parent, which is a blessing.

More Words of advice... from Mom

- Books are fun to read, and reading for fun does not make you a nerd.
- Nerds will win in the end. Highest paid athlete in 2010, $75 million in earnings and endorsements. Highest paid nerd, billions of dollars.
- Be yourself, you will like who you are.
- Open mind, open heart, and keep your eyes open so you do not miss a thing.
- Imagination is a good thing.
- Be an individual, not a member of the herd (no lemmings allowed).
- Outside is a beautiful place to be.
- Everyone has an opinion and you have the right not to listen.
- Lastly, it is okay to question.

Some words of advice from Dad...

- Remember not everyone is enlightened.
- Bullies are just sad pathetic people with low self esteem that make themselves feel better by harassing others to the point of cruelty. The way to frustrate a bully is not to react to them. When you are out of school and it has been twenty years or more bullies are nothing more than sad and pathetic, for the most part their ways did not get them far in life.
- High school is just a step we must all pass through, not the end all and be all, just a step. Bigger and better things are waiting. Time is cruel to some and kind to others.
- Give back through volunteering, it brings its own rewards.
- Get to know people, look beyond the physical appearance.
- Step out of your comfort zone, it's fun and enlightening.
- Risk and reward are always to be measured.
- Continue to educate yourself. Learning does not a nerd make but it is a path to understanding and enlightenment.
- Compassion is not a flaw but an asset.
- Have hobbies that get others involved, and take time to relax.
- Work requires commitment, not sacrifice.
- Be kind to animals, they need comfort too.
- Kiss first, sometimes it pays off.
- Learn to cook, do laundry, clean, budget, and shop. These are modern life survival skills.

- Lastly, for today, Dance to your own beat, forge a path and others will follow, be comfortable in your own skin, and you do not need to look for love, it usually finds you.

Advice from June 13th, 2011...

In part, this is an open letter to my future son and my grown children, but a few bits of advice on this morning.

- Only do things in "Gods name" if you get direct contact and explicit instructions.
- Terrorist are just cowards, like bullies and cockroaches, they scurry for the shadows when exposed in the light of day.
- Fun at the expense of others is cruelty.
- It is good to have friends, it is okay to need them occasionally, but it is bad to need to have friends. Friends who are only around when you are providing are not friends but moochers.
- Garbage in, garbage out.
- Trendsetters need affirmation that they are important, but they are just pathetic.
- Style is what you make of it.
- Do not be a lemming; you will eventually go over the proverbial cliff.
- Suicide is not an option, face every day, persevere, and grow with each challenge.
- Get an academic education, take classes in other disciplines, and find things you enjoy. Learning does not make you a nerd; it makes you a well-rounded individual.

__Words of Advice on June 16, 2011....__

Songs (by the original artist) that everyone should listen to at least once....

- World without Hero's by KISS
- Welcome to the Machine by Pink Floyd
- Simple Man by Lynard Skynard
- For Whom the Bell Tolls by Metallica
- Let it be by The Beatles
- The Entire Lost Christmas Eve by Trans Siberian Orchestra
- Immigrant Song by Led Zeppelin
- Renegade by Styx
- Ring of Fire by Johnny Cash
- Rock-n-Roll High School by The Ramones
- Lastly for today... Purple Rain by Prince

I know there are many more out there...

As I was going about my work today, I was thinking about some things I have heard over the years as good advice:

- Every man needs a good suit that fits well, along with a pair of wing tipped shoes to wear with the suit.
- Being a man does not mean you are a knuckle dragging, nose picking, butt scratching, beer swilling bore of a human being.
- It is okay to enjoy the arts, enlighten yourself with something artsy.
- It is okay to learn how to cook; most of the great chefs are men. Besides women enjoy a man who can cook for them once in a while.
- Work is work and play is play, never confuse the two.
- Always make time for your family; it pays its own rewards.
- Never stop learning new things, keeps the mind active and open to new things.
- You are never "too old" for anything.
- Take time to have a "tea party" or play cars with your children, they are only young for so long.
- Father does not always know best, he BS'es sometimes.
- The correct answer to "why?" is "because" at least according to Socrates.
- Religion, sex, and politics make for boring and heated conversation. Talk about something else, maybe hockey, or music.
- The party life is no life at all, just a slow slide towards death.
- Lastly, never play "pull my finger" with someone eating beans.

Thinking about a few things in the B.C. (before cell phones):

- You always told your parents where you were going and who you would be with along with their home phone number.
- When the lightening bugs came out it was time to report in at home.
- Bike safety was taught in Cub scouts, helmets were not even available for cyclist.
- Washing your hands with hot water and soap was good enough.
- Outside was your playroom regardless of weather. I spent many a winters' day building snow caves and many a rainy day in a yellow slicker playing in puddles.
- If you were doing something, you should not be doing a neighbor called your parents to inform them of your misdeeds.

Children are our future. Teach them well, teach them to think, teach them to be inquisitive, and teach them to think before they act, safety first.

A few things my child may never know:

- A TV without remotes
- Cassettes and even record stores.
- Life without a microwave, computer, cell phone, and cable TV
- Books actually printed on paper

Where does gravity fall?

A collection of poetry that I have written over the years for your enjoyment, sit back and read.

This first piece I wrote during my freshman year of college while taking a creative writing class. It is a tribute to friend of mine who died New Years Eve, six months after we had graduated high school.

Snowflakes

Why do they come?
Drifting, falling in downward flight,
To some they are welcome,
As they fall to earth tonight.
The whiteness has turned to grey,
The sky was blue,
"What might he say?"
Someone would ask you.
And now all is dark,
"For was it right?"
I have heard the meadowlark
Cry out it the night.
"Was it his time to die?
And soon shall I?"
Life goes on through the days,
He no longer walks by my side,
As we wander through the fields of hay.
This brother of mine took a ride,
To the worlds above the ground.
In the time of night,
One might look around,
And see that he was right.
Peace be with you,

Brother of mine,
You venture to a world of new,
Where you will remember the time of nine.
"Weep not for me,"
Says he, "Remember what it is to be."

Another poem from that same time...
Self Portrait #1
Only the looking glass can show the three,
Me, myself, and I.
Stone cold he is,
Diabolical in every way.
Savage and lustful,
Cold and calculating,
The mind is his realm.
Only his reality is true,
Pain and comfort control him.
His doings are the effects of the others.
He knows no love nor hatred,
Only the consequences,
The body is his realm.
Gentle he is,
Chivalry is his code,
Love and caring are his actions.
He is spiritual,
Seeking out knowledge and truth,
The soul is his realm.
These three,
Me, myself, and I,
Are the body, mind, and soul.
None can live without the others,
All are strong,
And yet all are weak.
The mind and soul struggle,
To control the body,
And it seems,
One shall become strong,

While the other is weak.
And so on the two battle...
Look into the mirror and see
Which is strong and which is weak.

The following is a collection of untitled works that I have written over the last twenty-five or so years.

Untitled #1

When the moon breaks the horizon,
When the night begins to gather,
You'll find us there,
At the edge of your vision,
Sliding in and out of the shadows.
Wolf brothers we are
And will be,
The guardians of the night,
The protectors of the innocents,
The watchers,
The warriors,
The pack.

Untitled #2

Minstrel of fate play a new song for me,
I have heard your songs all my life,
And yet they seem ever new.
I pray for a sad song,
A song of sorrow,
One of sickness,
Of pestilence, of death.
For I cannot explain these feelings,
Inside of me,
The pain and distrust.
I hurt not for myself
But for others in this world
Whom are without family, food or home.
The ones who daily call out to you
For the song of mourning and death.
Hear me O minstrel let all who sit in this land
At one time or another with a gluttonous, hedonistic, pish
posh view,
Feel the pain of the others.
Play your song of harmony, balance, and peace...

Untitled #3
What do you do when you think
The whole world is laughing at you?
Do you cry?
Or take a walk and wonder why?
Am I small and insignificant?
No!
Can I fly above
And conquer them all?
Yes!
The sounds of the world
Form music in my mind,
A melody that I pull from the air,
That makes me strong with time.
Just being alone in the crowd
With a song in your mind
That you sing to yourself
Is just being alone in the crowd
And nothing is wrong.

Untitled #4
Life,
A two bit whore in heat,
Always looking for some john
Who will give her more than she deserves.
Five, ten, and if she's lucky maybe a twenty.
But all she wants
Is a piece of action
Your body,
Your life.
Full of disease and death.

Untitled #5
Hear the snow
Watching it drift down
From the sky
Piling up
Around my feet
Deep it is
Cleansing me
And the world too
Good it is

This is the poem that will one day become a song of mine by the same title.

Travelling man
It seems like I have been here before
But I don't know why
For every town on the road looks the same
Only the faces
Faces seem to change
But I think I've been here before
But I don't know why
Last night I was in this town along the road
All the faces seem familiar
But I don't know why
There was a girl
Whom seemed to know me
But they always do
Maybe I've been here before
But I don't know why
For every town on the road looks the same
The road has been so long
Every inn seems like home
Maybe someday I'll be caught by a travelling woman
Then the road won't seem so long anymore
Maybe we will settle down
And start a family
But right now I am still rolling down the road
The road has been to long
And it is wearing me down
I am going to lie down
And get some sleep maybe when I wake up
I will be in the next town again.

Infinite Odyssey
We had nothing to do but start a time,
A time with a beginning
And yet without an end,
But yet it had an end,
Without a beginning.
It was our odyssey
Without any dimension.
It was a time
When world were created
And those that existed were destroyed
See that star the one flickering red
Tomorrow it will be gone in a flash
Here we are travelling like Ulysses
On an odyssey in space
Could it be that we will not see home again
In twenty millennia
Can you hear her?
The siren of space
She is luring you to an airless grave
That no one will find until the end of time.
It is only a dream
Space is not real
It is just call of ages old
To search the heavens
In our time of discovery
The power of time will be lost
To those who are unready
We shall lead the way
On this space odyssey
The time

The dimension
The end of the worlds
Pilot
Lead the way the in forgotten time
Since time no longer exist
We need not worry about being late
Since supper will not be ready
Lead us to the end for there was no beginning.

Which way for a Witch?
Which way for a witch?
Boil, boil, toil, and trouble,
Is it double?
Dancing in the moonlight?
Or sunshine in the glade?
Carousing at a faire,
Or fairly carousing?
Turn a charm,
Or taking a charming turn?
Life's questions must be met,
Head on in this unwitchy world.
For solitary selves we must be,
To survive amongst the flock.
Eagles in a world of ducks
Soaring above constraints
Of ignorance and injustice.
So?
Which way for a witch?

This last piece was another ode to a friend who died.
Death of a friend
She was more loyal to me
Than most women in my life
I saved her once from death
But was powerless this time
In the end it was right, euthanasia
For my friend
She need not suffer anymore
For she had done enough
Good bye my friend
And remember not to pee on the tree of life
My most loyal four legged friend,
Maxine.

Journey of Discovery

I do not usually write on the subject of religion but this morning I was inspired in the predawn hours to write about my own journey of discovery, my journey to find the spiritual me in the sea of religions. So let the story begin... The first amendment of the constitution guarantees the freedom of religion among other freedoms. The religious right takes this freedom as only specifying freedom of Christian religious beliefs as they determine the spirit of the amendment not the letter of the amendment. One must remember it says freedom of religion not freedom of Christian belief/religion.

My story is similar to many children growing up in a small town where the church your family belongs to says as much about their religious beliefs as well as social status. Church on Sunday was not only your weekly dose of soul saving from fire and damnation as a social event. At the age of thirteen, I went through the necessary course of religious immersion after which you are now an "adult" member of the church. It is one of those milestone moments in life followed by a mandatory celebration at your house in which your parents get to show off. Lots of cards and gifts (money too) for you lots of social dancing for your parents as they use you to show they are successful as parents.

This point actually started me thinking about where I fit in the cosmos and if the flavor of Christianity I was now a part of was right for me. This journey started at that point and continued for quite some time beyond my teenage years and way into adulthood. I did the typical things as many do, I belonged to a church sponsored youth group, belonged to a Boy Scout troop (where I achieved the Rank of Eagle Scout), reading any book I could get my hands on about different beliefs, took several comparative religion/philosophy classes in college, and experimented by visiting many different churches and beliefs. One defining moment for me was my Eagle Scout board of review where I was posed the question "Did I believe in god?" My answer was "I believe in a higher power" and that answer satisfied the questioner. Yes there is a god but not specifically of any one belief for all we know God (with a big G) is all to all people just called different names, prayed to differently, and responds differently to each but accepts the praise no matter the name it (I find it hard to believe god is male or female so "it" is the proper pronoun) is called.

I have always had a strong connection to the earth not in the sense of a farmer but in the sense of calmness when in the woods, working in the garden, with animals, and when working with the bounties of nature (cooking and such). One day on a break from classes, I decided to relax by taking a walk through Black Hawk State park in Rock Island, Illinois. Scattered along the trails there are benches for one to stop, sit, and rest. Before starting down the trails, I found a suitable walking stick and headed into the park, stopping at one of the benches deep in the park for a rest I had a moment of epiphany. Sitting there relaxing and listening to the birds sing, and the scamper of animals through the underbrush and trees just coming to leaf; the sounds of the traffic flowing by the parks edge seemed to fade away from the cacophony of wild noises. In that moment I was opened up to the wider universe and ideas/information began to flow in, at that point I found my religious path in life. There was not a visitation from an emissary of whatever being just a moment of clarity where the puzzle pieces I had suddenly assembled into a larger picture and nudged me down a path of my own choosing.

Following the path that I discovered at times can be difficult, difficult to explain to the unenlightened and narrow minded, but as with any belief these little test of faith only help to solidify and define my beliefs. It is my personal opinion that religious beliefs are a personal and private relationship between you and your chosen deity. If you choose to do it in a collective manner (i.e. at church, temple, or mosque) then that is your right and if you choose to do it in quietness of your home that is your right also. When asked what my religion is I often respond with "agnostic" because whether you call that being Jehovah, Allah, Yahweh, Brahman, or something else they all are part of the pantheon, all worthy of praise and prayer to; and getting back to the topic they all are part of my belief they just represent different aspects of the same greater being.

The aspect I follow is the aspect more closely associated with nature, often the path is more associated with women than men are but that does not mean men are excluded. With this path I have tried to associate with groups of like pathed people but have always found the internal politics of those groups to be detrimental, as with any group when all are equal and some are more equal than others conflict and clicks within the group can cause the group to implode. Also not everyone in the same faith has the same direction in mind for the group and after several attempts to join a community of like minds and faith I settled on being a solitary practitioner. It does not mean I shy away from others who follow the same path I just do not practice our faith in a community setting.

As the circle comes around in full in this discussion, I am glad I live in the country I live in because it does offer the ability to explore ones belief without persecution from the government. That does not mean you will be free from persecution by your fellow citizens, not everyone is enlightened or open to alternative beliefs different from their own, but it means you have the right to practice as you choose as long as it does not violate any criminal laws (sacrifices of living animals prohibited). The religious right needs to be reminded that on the whole only thirty-five percent of the world population can be characterized as following some form of Christianity, which leaves approximately over four billion people having a non-christian belief.

To all the right wing zealots who claim the US was founded as a Christian nation by religious, church-going men...

Please say hello to a few of the Founding Fathers.

History, I believe, furnishes no example of a priest-ridden people maintaining a free civil government. -Thomas Jefferson, 1813

An alliance or coalition between Government and religion cannot be too carefully guarded against. -James Madison, 1822

"The Government of the United States of America is not, in any sense, founded on the Christian religion." -Treaty of Tripoli, signed by John Adams, 1797

"As to Jesus of Nazareth, my opinion of whom you particularly desire, I think the system of morals and his religion, as he left them to us, the best the world ever saw or is likely to see, but I apprehend it has received various corrupt changes, and I have, with most of the present Dissenters of England, some doubts as to his divinity." -Benjamin Franklin, 1790

Of all the systems of religion that ever were invented, there is none more derogatory to the Almighty, more unedifying to man, more repugnant to reason, and more contradictory in itself, than this thing called Christianity. Too absurd for belief, too impossible to convince, and too inconsistent for practice, it renders the heart torpid, or produces only atheists and fanatics. -Thomas Paine, 1795

The Measure of Success

What do you measure success with money, power, prestige/fame, the people you surround yourself with, the people you know, the things you have, is it by your achievements, your position in society, the school you attended or your children attend, or a combination of many things. Success is an intrinsic qualifier, defined by the individual and in part by the larger society of which that individual resides.

Too many mark success by the amount of money they have, even knowing that when they are gone someone else will be spending that money they earned. Too often, the next generation takes that money for granted, an entitlement of wealth and assume, sometimes wrongly, that it will always be there. A few will work to add to the wealth but most will spend it freely since it was not their sweat that accumulated the coin. History is ripe with those that tried to take their wealth with them into the next life, so wealth is out.

Again, what is your measure of success? Power, power leads to corruption, power leads to a misplaced superiority complex, and it seems power and wealth goes hand in hand. Look at the Catholic Church, one of the wealthiest entities on the planet and one of the most powerful with an estimated one-billion devoted followers. The very same entity that tells its malnourished and undereducated parishioners in parts of the world to continue to be fruitful and multiply even though they barely can feed themselves while you never see a priest that is starving unless they are paying a penance. Doing things in the name of religion can hide a multitude of wrongs as long as it is the dominate belief. The very same church that for millennia tried to control or eliminate any who would not bend to the "will of god" or tried to progress scientific endeavors in Europe for fear that an enlightened and educated population would have no use for spirituality. Life without hope is no life at all.

Again, what is your measure of success? Fame or prestige, fame is fleeting and prestige is a short step from power. What was "it" today can be tomorrows has beens, ask any child star that could not make it as an adult. Prestige can be narrow in scope and limited by the field of the endeavor, many a Nobel Prize winning scientist is forgotten by the news after their brief exposure but others may not so easily dismiss them in their field of expertise. Fame and prestige are as capricious as the summer breeze and as fleeting as mayfly's life.

How do I measure success? By the happiness, I find in life, by a job well done, by the love and respect of friends, family, and peers, and by simple pleasures. I used to think success was all about the accumulation of wealth. Working long hours at an unrewarding but high paying job that allowed me to provide expensive things for my family but left me little time to enjoy those nice toys and in the end I was left empty and hollow feeling. Today I measure success by the goals I set for myself, by the things I create with my own hands, and by sharing with others. Cooking and enjoying the results of the culinary arts is a measure of success, nothing is better than a home cooked meal and there is no better measure of success than the lack of leftovers.

As I look over my life, I find what true successes were and they were all the result of perseverance, patience, practice, sustained effort, and goal orientated in nature.

Eagle Scout, Bachelors degree, Masters Degree, publishing my first book, and many more, I often measure success by the little things in life, spending time with friends and family, I find people who take their wealth and all that goes with it and use it to help others to be more successful than those that do nothing but accumulate wealth for the sake of having more.

More on the election process

Listening to the Republican candidates in Florida and hearing one candidate call another a liberal on the issue of gun control makes me think of what is my opinion on gun control. What is my position? Good question but not an easy answer, therein lays the crux of the matter, like most issues it is not as black and white as everyone would like it to be.

So here it is:

- Gun ownership? Yes. Set smart limits on the number of firearms an individual can own.
- Limit the types of firearms owned? Yes. Here is the tough part, the part that gets both the NRA and anti-gun advocates riled up.
  - Pistols, yes, limit to nine shot clips and to single shot/semi-automatic, full automatic pistols should be illegal.
  - Revolvers, yes, classic handgun, either single action or double action are allowed. Pistols and revolvers are great for home protection and target shooting.
  - Shotguns, yes, but limit to the single shot or double barrel variety, no private citizen needs to have a shot gun that hold more than two shells. Shotguns have a purpose, hunting or trap shooting; pump action and multi-shot clip capable shotguns do not have a purpose outside of the military and law enforcement.
  - Rifles, yes, bolt action and single shot rifles designed for hunting or target shooting are okay. What is not okay are the commercial grade knock downed assault style rifles like the AR-15, these

non-military grade rifles are easily converted from a semi-automatic to a fully automatic rifle have no real purpose other than to be used against other people and should not be owned by private citizens.

- Open carry and Concealed carry? Yes and yes, although smart limits need to be set. The obvious ones are safe zones around schools, minimum of one-thousand feet, and similar safe zones around government buildings, courthouses, hospitals, and colleges/universities.

Firearm ownership is a core belief and a constitutional guarantee, the right to bear arms. Responsible firearm ownership and responsible laws and enforcement of those laws by a responsible government is what is needed, unfortunately special interest groups on both sides of the issue make responsible laws not possible and put our law enforcement professionals at a disadvantage especially in high crime areas where drugs and violence go hand in hand. Firearms have purposes, primarily for hunting (another whole issue in itself), target and trap shooting, home and property protection, and personal protection but as I stated earlier not every firearm meets these criteria and that is the important aspect. What constitutes responsible laws by a responsible government that are enforceable? Federalization or standardization of laws across the country that allow the private citizen to own firearms but limit the type and number of firearms that citizens can own. Responsible laws should include waiting periods for the purchase of all types of firearms, better and more thorough background checks, and psychological testing.

Conservative, Moderate, or Liberal, all are politicians

I am not running for office but if I was here are more thoughts on the process...

It is that time of year again, when the political debates start up, the primaries get rolling, the candidates are out kissing babies and shaking hands, and labels are being bandied about like weapons. Are you a Conservative, Moderate, or Liberal? Does it really matter? All are politicians looking to fill a niche to get votes and be elected, but in the end, they are all politicians. What would be truly refreshing would be someone to label themselves as a patriot, an independent, free of political party affiliations. Would they be elected? Who knows, as long as their platform seems reasonable and presented in a logical manner, again who knows. I would like to someone run on a platform of term limits, campaign finance reform, and further limits on special interests and lobbyist. If someone actually proposed these ideas, the other candidates would label them as socialist or communist because they sound anti-American but they are what America truly needs.

The President said it himself, there is a disconnect between those politicians in Washington D.C. and the rest of the country. Labels are powerful in the political arena, labels define who you are, who your adversaries are, and who your allies are, and in large part where you stand on the issues of the day. Another thing I would like to see is the end of attack ads against other candidates, if you do not have something nice to say do not say anything at all. Last refreshing thought, a candidate who takes no money from special interest groups and limits all contributions to no more than fifty dollars. Part of the reform process would have to come from the media and news outlets by offering free advertising space to all candidates regardless of affiliation, but hey, there is big money is political season advertising.

If I were to run for Office

First of all, why does anyone want to run for office? Several simple reasons:

- Job security, it is nearly impossible to vote out incumbents unless they do something drastically wrong or there is a massive shift in public open.
- Great benefits, at least on the state and federal level, the best that tax payers can buy.
- The best perks that lobbyist can buy.
- Lastly, at least at the federal level, an easy workweek, think of this, last year both houses of congress were actually only in session eighty days, which is only sixteen weeks of work out of fifty-two. By comparison, the average U.S. worker worked fifty-one weeks in 2011, mostly due to the higher amount of "part time" employees who work without benefits.

So what would my platform be? The platform is education reform, job creation through small business and local economies of scale, campaign finance reform and congressional term limits. I would focus on these issues, leaving alone abortion (until the Supreme Court says otherwise is legal and no man has any right to tell a woman otherwise), gay marriage or civil unions are doing well on their own and gaining momentum, taxes are an old and tired song, redistribution of wealth will get you laughed off the stage, reducing redundancy in government is the equivalent killing the golden goose, improvement of social services and reducing waste in the system is another golden egg that is off limits, and immigration reform which is another tired old song.

- Education reform, how is this going to work and why do we need it? Let me start with a few anecdotes on our education system. A few years ago I read a Bill Wundrum column on an eighth grade graduation test that several of us read and determined (all of us had advanced degrees) that we would be hard pressed to pass certain portions of the test. Add in to this a test booklet we found cleaning out my great aunts house; she was a schoolteacher in one of the last one-room schoolhouses in Illinois, of similar design and complexity. My father, who was still teaching at the time, said the test was harder than the G.E.D. test at the time. A sad note on the dumbing down of America, and the decline of our prominence in the world as the bastion of higher learning and innovation, consider this, Japan graduates more engineers from its universities than any other nation whereas the U.S. graduates more lawyers then the rest of the G20 combined. At one time an eighth grade diploma meant you could find a job and provide for your family, a high school diploma was an automatic entry into a factory job, a bachelors degree meant you could teach your area of expertise to primary and secondary students, a masters enabled you to teach at a community college, and a doctoral degree meant you could do research and teach at a university. As we have progressed we have done away with the eighth grade graduation, a high school diploma or equivalent qualifies you for manual labor and non management service industry jobs, a bachelors means you are trainable, a masters means you can teach, and a doctoral means you can do research. So how would I reform education? There are three basic steps to the reformation of our education system. One, do away with standardized testing with the exception of the ACT and SAT, which are used for college admission, more time is spent in the classroom teaching to perform on whatever state test is being used. Students should be able to pass knowledge test at three points in a student's primary and secondary education career, at eighth grade including knowledge of the state constitution, in high school passing a U.S. constitution test, and after the sophomore year to see if the student is ready to graduate and progress on to a community college or university. At this point students will have two options, to continue to prepare for a university or to begin learning a trade skill. If this sounds similar to a European educational system then you are right, too many students graduate high school without any marketable skills and are fit only for minimum wage slave jobs in fast food and big box retail.

- Job creation through small business and local economies of scale, small business is the backbone of our economy, part of this is reforming the tax code to make it more lucrative to be an owner operator by raising the income level where taxes are to be collected thus leaving more money in the pockets of the working class. No taxes collected until income passes sixty-thousand dollars per person or one-hundred-thousand dollars for a family or small business. By putting money back into the pockets of the working class you have the opportunity to increase the amount of disposable income moving through the economy and by focusing on the local businesses you put money back into U.S. business and not into large multinational companies that may or may not keep that money here in the U.S.A. I am not xenophobic but charity starts at home before it goes abroad.

- Campaign finance reform and congressional term limits, are actually easy, simply put a limit on the amount of money that can be raised and spent, eliminate political action groups, limit campaign donations to one-hundred dollars per individual or group, and eliminate political parties all candidates stand on their own platform not some amorphous political parties platform catering to the fringes to appease the middle. Term limits are also easy, limit the time a person can serve in congress to twenty years of total time between both houses. It should be a sign that term limits are necessary when the average age of a senator is over sixty-five, an age when most people are retiring from work and not looking to extend their career another six years. We have term limits on the President, some states have term limits for their governor, and some cities have term limits for their mayor, why then are we afraid to set term limits for congress. Our founding fathers never envisioned a member of congress dying in office due to extreme old age and serving over forty years in office. What our founding fathers envisioned were civic-minded gentleman landowners as senators and representatives, giving a short period of public service for the betterment of the country, not professional politicians giving an entire adult lifetime of service for the betterment of their pockets. Is it sad that of the top ten wealthiest members of congress, nine of them are democrats including the number one spot.

What prevents me from running for office? Money, I am not a fortunate one or a millionaires son. No one who runs for state level or federal level office does so without deep pockets or deep-pocketed friends.

First random thoughts of 2012

- It always amazes me at the ignorance people display
  when it comes to technology. I can understand people of
  a certain generation having difficulties understanding the
  functionality of technological devices. It is the under 50
  crowd that always makes me shake my head and wonder
  why some choose to remain ignorant and not learn the
  proper applications and uses for current technology. The
  other aspect of this why would you allow your child to use
  the device unsupervised, and then blame the company or
  service when your child places charges on your credit
  card. As a parent, you have a level of responsibility, a
  level of required supervision, and a level of educating
  your child on what is in your beliefs considered acceptable
  behavior. Blaming a company or service for what your
  child does is irresponsible on your behalf. Where were
  you when the child was accessing something you thought
  they should not? People always assume that what was
  being accessed is the party to blame. Wrong. Websites
  cannot "see" who is accessing them, they cannot peer into
  the mind to see if something is acceptable, and they do
  not check to see if the person presenting the payment is
  actually the cardholder. Day in and day out, I hear
  people whine about how they did not know that "such and
  such" works a particular way or how a service functions.
  I have one thing to say: Take time to educate yourself
  and accept a certain level of responsibility. Ignorance is
  no excuse, and blaming someone else for your lack of
  action is the equivalent of "the dog ate my homework."
  Your lack of responsibility and ignorance does not illicit
  concern on the part of the customer service personnel, on

occasion be an adult and take the blame for your lack of action.

- With the start of the Primaries for the Republican nomination I cannot say this enough, "Who really cares?" both political parties are so out of touch with the average citizen, with the 99%, that watching the political jockeying is almost as entertaining as watching a documentary on the mating habits of the Venezuelan giant slug. Do you want to see real debates, real political discussion, and candidates that the "Joe Average" citizen can associate with then push for reforms in campaign financing by placing limits on fundraising and spending by the candidates, eliminate P.A.C. (Political Action Committees more commonly known as political parties), and eliminate third party political advertising (no more adds by such and such group for political transparency).

- I know I have commented on this before, but outside of LSU and Alabama fans, who cares? The BCS National Title Sham is more fuel for the fire of a playoff system in Division I-A football. After watching great bowl games, particularly the Rose Bowl and the Fiesta Bowl, there were three teams (Wisconsin, Oregon, or Oklahoma State) that should have been playing LSU. All three were conference champions as opposed to Alabama who is not a conference champion. If the game goes again as a low scoring, defensive struggle, and LSU wins again then all that is proven is the first meeting was a clear indicator as to the differences between the two teams, otherwise if Alabama wins it will prove the adage that it is difficult to beat the same team twice in one season. LSU must win for there to be a clear National Champion otherwise both

Oregon and OSU have cases for being the BCS champions by virtue of their bowl victories. Enough said, to the NCAA, dump the BCS system, consolidate the 121 D-IA Schools into eight football only conferences, have conference title games, then have an eight-team playoff of conference champions for a true national championship.

It is Just My Opinion...

- Being a curmudgeon is just saying what everyone else is thinking.
- If you are doing things in "God's name" you had better have had direct and verifiable contact along with set of written instructions. Last time this happened, people wandered around the desert for forty years before settling down.
- Why do good people have no luck at all?
- If you tell an OWS protestor to get a job you had better be willing to vacate yours.
- The Bills Of Rights are just that, RIGHTS.
- When did the exercising of your rights become a full contact sport?
- Real life is often stranger than fiction.
- Why is it when you need a little help to get back on your feet people who control that help treat you like second class citizens.
- I may not have much but it is mine and leave it alone.
- Why is it the people who should not reproduce do so like rabbits and those who would be good parents can't?
- When did manners go out of style?
- If you insist on driving under the speed limit in the left lane then you should not be amazed when people tell you that you are number one in sign language.
- I could care less if the NBA never plays again, just another case of the rich arguing over how to get even richer.
- In 1776, acts of civil disobedience sparked a revolution, it can happen again.

- If Politicians were required to work like the average American, our government would run like it should not like it does. Our founding fathers envisioned gentleman congressmen serving for a period of time before retiring to manage their affairs not serving so long as to die while in office.
- I do not want to be President; I want to be a Senator. No term limits, easy hours, and once you are an incumbent great job security.
- Tea party, just another name for pissed off republicans.
- Sanity is only a state of mind.
- Everyone deserves the right to be legally joined in a matrimonial union, so says the Association of Divorce Lawyers, but really, everyone does deserve the chance to be legally joined with that special person.

Quick Notes for New Years Eve, Last Comments of 2011

- NFL and the NBA have labor issues that threaten the season, one phrase: "College Sports," no labor stoppages in the NCAA.
- Bowl season comes and a great variety of games but too many mediocre teams are playing in the bowls.
- Once again the National Title game is a rematch of a regular season game between conference rivals, how boring, and besides 'Bama is not even a conference champion. LSU should be playing OSU, not a conference rival. It is high time for a playoff system.
- It has been a year of big personal changes, new job, new baby, and a new grandbaby on the way.
- As the political year begins in earnest, do we really care who wins in Iowa and New Hampshire. Nothing really matters until the convention is over and we know who the Tea baggers are going to push down our throats. It is time to eliminate political parties; they are the detriment to passing legislation. Our congressional representatives need to vote with the welfare of their constituents in mind and not like lemmings with what their party leaders are saying is the "correct" option.
- Like with computers, congress should remember this phrase: "Garbage in, garbage out."
- Looking at the list of celebrities that died over the past year, some deaths were related to age and disease, some by accident, and some by substance abuse/overuse. The ones who died by substance abuse/overuse are just reminders for the rest of us, cautionary tales with no golden endings.

- Remember tonight is the night all the amateurs come out to party. Be safe and do not drink and drive.
- Lastly, another year passes and we remember those lost to us. I will raise a toast to Jody "Joe" Mateka, gone now twenty-six years as of this night and Jaymz Leland Hoburg gone now twenty-one years, among the many who have now passed.

Being a new dad once again

It is interesting being a new dad once again, considering my youngest is twenty years old now. First let me start by emphasizing that my fiancé and I were not expecting to have children, we thought we would grow old together as a pair of empty nesters, for doctors had told her that she would never successfully get pregnant, meaning carrying the fetus to term. She had had two miscarriages in her adult life, neither going past eight weeks of pregnancy. After the first sonogram, showing the fetus was attached to the uterus every day became a miracle. When we found out the baby's gender, our thoughts turned to giving it a name. Naming a child is not easy, you have to make sure of the spelling, how it will be pronounced, and its meaning and uniqueness. With each doctor's appointment, the upcoming birth of our child became closer to being a reality. My fiancé could not enjoy being pregnant due to the stress of gestational diabetes and a tightly controlled diet, being older meaning a high risk pregnancy, school (she is a nursing student), and the fact this was new territory for her. Each day, as I said earlier, became a minor miracle. Then at five months came the hard decisions if the genetic testing would show any abnormalities, we were lucky, no abnormalities, onward the pregnancy progressed.

Then at the thirty-nine week appointment, her blood pressure started to creep up, the doctor said within two days we would have a baby. We were told to check in to the hospital so the process could be started and within twenty-four hours, we would have a newborn baby in our arms. Of course, the night we were to check in was a busy night in labor and delivery, after a nearly four-hour wait we were in a labor and delivery room and the birthing process begun. Everything was going well until the process stalled out when she was a nine centimeters, the baby had failed to enter the birth canal and a caesarian section was now necessary.

My thoughts drifted back to a day twenty-one years earlier when my first son was born and subsequently died due to a prolapsed umbilical cord (the cord was wrapped around his neck and strangled him, he was born brain dead and died within minutes) and the stress started to mount. I had to show a brave face and erase my fears to support my fiancé, to make sure she did not crack under the pressure. So far, the baby was fine and not in distress. Off she went to the operating room to be prepared for surgery and I was dressed in cap, gown, and booties to be by her side. With a screen to block of the view of her belly, and me sitting by her head listened to the doctor and assistant go through the process to remove the baby. Then we heard "we are removing the baby from the uterus," followed by a scream any heavy metal singer would be proud of, out came our son into the world. Over the screen the doctor flashed us our healthy child and the stress drained out of us, he made here and in good health.

Now the old and rusty skills were coming back, changing diapers, feeding, holding, burping, etc. and were being put to use. Right now, the biggest issue is getting on the baby's schedule as to feeding and sleeping but as a once again new parent I am up for the challenge; I am doing my part so my fiancé can continue her studies, and taking some of the stress off her. Every day is now an adventure, welcome my son, welcome to the machine.

How can we create change?

Change is terrifying. Change is necessary. Change can bring progress. Change does not lead to stagnation. Change can be easy. Change can be difficult. We can accept change or we can fight change but change is inevitable. You can be part of the solution and facilitate the change or you can be part of the problem and be why the change is happening. Change does not mean the end of things as we know them, change is the ushering in of a new era. Change can revitalize us or change can demoralize us only if we succumb to the despair that comes with loss. Change is a force for creativity, for forging a new tomorrow, and for enlightenment. Change is the only constant. Our universe is constantly changing. The seasons change. Change happens daily as darkness becomes light and as the daylight succumbs to the night. We can accept change or we can stagnate. Whichever path we choose we will change, the only question will be, "is the change of our own accord or are we being forced to change?"

What does the "Occupy Wall Street" movement want? What needs to change? How can we facilitate change? How can we make sure that the change benefits every one of us? How can we use change to prevent a repeat of what brought us to this point? What are the steps to the change? Will the change actually create change or will it just obfuscate the current situation. How can we lend our voices to the change? I love my country but I dislike what those who hold the power do with that power and I fear that there is no difference between the two parties; the only difference is the packaging.

I do not begrudge those that achieve their success through hard work and perseverance. I do have an issue with those who achieve their success through smoke and mirrors or use the hard work of others to further their own ambitions and wealth.

Some insights into WHAT needs to change:

- Term limits on congress. I do not want to be president; I want to be a senator. The senate is where the real power in American politics is vested. To remove an incumbent senator is nearly impossible. No senator should serve long enough that two generations of voters have been born while they are in office. Our founding fathers envisioned a congress of public servants that would serve for a limited time then retire to their private life not individuals serving for the rest of their lives.

- Checks and balances put in place to prevent the financial collapse from repeating. We need to make sure that every citizen has faith in the financial industry. We need a strong financial industry to fuel the reawakening of American industry and the job market. We need the financial industry providing financing to small businesses, which are the backbone of American industry and provide the greatest number of jobs available in the workforce.

- We need congress voting their consciences and not along party lines. We need an end to partisan politics, our elected officials were elected to represent us, the voters and constituents, not pander to the elitist special interest groups backed by corporations. The difference between a politician and a patriot is a politician will do what will further their career and a patriot will do what is best for their country. As a country we need more patriots and fewer politicians, it is time for voters to quit being apathetic and express their opinions. Remember, if you do not exercise your right to vote then you have no right to complain about the job those elected are doing.

Randomness of thought...

Why is it when budget cuts come around education and educational programs are always on the chopping block? Is it any wonder why our children are failing behind the rest of the world? The United States used to be the pinnacle of education, now we are slowly sliding down the scale. Our funding of education needs to be a priority, fund the arts as well as the sciences, and quit pouring additional monies into sports programs. Path to education reform: Institute a uniform dress code, studies have found that public schools that have a "uniform" dress code have test scores rise over time, less instances of classroom disruptions, less instances of bullying, and students report less stress about going to school. Unfortunately, make interscholastic sports a "pay to play" system, if your student wants to play a particular sport you have to foot part of the bill. This is already happening around the country in smaller school districts that are strapped to fund regular classroom activities. Increase tax levies for education, educating the next generation should be priority number one not number one-thousand. Lastly, state academies for Math and Science, and for the Arts. Some areas and states already do this but every state needs to do this. Our education system is already one where the "haves" are getting more and the "haves not" are getting less; spending needs to equalize across the system.

Is sexting cheating? A better question is: Why would you want to send compromising pictures to someone else, who is not your partner, for the purpose of receiving similar pictures in return? In the internet age things can get spread rather quickly.

All religions attempt to explain our existence on this rock. Why should we argue over who is right when all boil down to "live a conscientious life" and "do no harm."
Your failure to act accordingly does not create an emergency for me or prompt me to take action.

If you sign up for something read the fine print, it is there for a reason.
Living healthy is expensive; no wonder we have become a nation of overweight couch potatoes.

Heard a commentator on the radio talking about if older generations had been "green" we would have less problems with the environment today. His comments did remind me of days gone by and how we were "green" then...I remember when beverages came in glass bottles and you returned those bottles for credit. I remember when the state of Iowa started giving $.05 cents refund on glass bottles and aluminum cans. You were also charged that refund amount extra at purchase. Doing a little research, in 1940, the average family produced about two tons of garbage per year, in 2000; the average family produced about ten tons of garbage per year. I remember when groceries left the store in paper bags, and those bags were the basis for art projects amongst other things. We walked or rode our bikes to school, the grocery store, to our friend's house, and not had mom drive us. I remember our garden, which provided fresh vegetables for the summer; and the canning and pickling of said vegetables in the fall; along with homemade grape jelly from our grape arbor. Learning to cook, pre-made and prepackaged foods were expensive and rather bland tasting. I used to think TV dinners (good ole Swansons meals in a tin tray) were an inducement for being well behaved for the

sitter. Water came from the faucet or a fountain not a plastic bottle with some exotic name on it for a price.
What is wrong with this picture: 187 Teachers, Principles and other school administrators in the Atlanta, GA public school system are under investigation for manipulating standardized test results to show the school was helping the students improve as shown by the raising of test scores. Here is a symptom of a larger issue when it comes to handing out money to schools for the "increases" in test results, why would a school district need to do this? Simple answer: Our education system is floundering and needs to be overhauled in such a manner that our standards match the expectations. Think of these two facts: 1. Japan graduates more engineering students from their universities than any other nation. 2. The United States graduates more lawyers than all the European Union combined (roughly the same population).

Heard a discussion on the new law in Illinois on Civil Unions. Kudos to Illinois for tackling the issue of gay marriage in the right sense. The Civil Union is no different from a marriage both individuals have the same rights and protections under the law as any heterosexual couple has and by that standard, the marriage certificates in Illinois starting in 2012 will all be called Civil Union certificates. The State has separated marriage from civil union by using the language "the state has a right to grant the formation of a legal union between two consenting adults" and hands the matter of a marriage back to where it belongs, religious organizations. Marriage is a religious matter while the legal formation of a union is matter for the state, separate and different, one is for legal issues, and one is to satisfy one's religious beliefs.

Surfing again through the radio channels came across a discussion on the beginnings of the push to repeal the anti-polygamy laws in the U.S., which were created to specifically target the Mormon movement and part of the government agreement, which allowed Utah to become a state. Oddly enough the U.S. is one of the few G20 nations that have anti-polygamy laws, most countries do not specifically address it as a crime but place limits on the number of adult relationships within the family unit. Remembering what a Political Science professor had once said that the laws in the U.S. had their roots in the Puritan social beliefs and our national views were shaped by as such the religious right of center view on life in general. Work hard (nothing wrong with that), family first (nothing wrong again) and place god above all else and god's law (I do have a problem with this. Which god?) were the basic puritan tenets. Personally, I do not have a problem with polygamy or polyandry (wife with multiple husbands) as long as all parties involved are consenting adults and agree to the situation. It becomes a problem when one of the parties is neither consenting nor in agreement and is forced/coerced into the situation at hand. There is a movement called "polyamorous" which is very similar to polygamy but where two individuals have a legal marriage and the third (or extra partners) is a willing/consenting participant. The home situation is very similar to a polygamist household, shared family/household responsibilities and separate sexual relations among the adult members. This skirts the legal ramifications, meaning illegal polygamist activities, by not referencing the tertiary relationship as husband/wife but as partners, and all children of the household are taken care of and treated with equality. In some way as a nation, we need to look in the mirror and see if we like the face staring back at us. In our national discourse, we talk about freedoms but do we really want to grant them? As in the phrase "Life, liberty and the pursuit of happiness," are we willing to grant fringe groups equal rights or are we just blowing smoke?

Now with college football back in full swing it is time to take a swipe at the failed BCS championship format of D1-A schools. Here is an alternative (and please read all the way through before forming and opinion): An eleven-team playoff system. Why eleven teams? There are eleven D1-A football conferences and in this system only conference champions (as determined by each conference through championship game or round robin play) would qualify, all independent teams would not qualify no matter how good their record is (Sorry Notre Dame you need to join the Big East for all sports not for all sports but football) and which university they are. Here is how the playoff would go: First round six teams would play, eliminating three, after which there would eight teams left. Next rounds would go as follows round of eight (quarterfinals), round of four (semifinals), championship game. A total of ten games to be televised (imagine the dollars the NCAA would generate for this system) and would add a maximum of four games to any college teams' schedule. Rules to add/change: limit teams to eleven game seasons plus conference championship game, eliminate games between D1-A (FBS) schools and D1-AA (FCS) schools, and eliminate automatic bowl bids (set bowl eligibility at minimum of eight wins). With 33 bowl games each year, use some of the lower tier bowls as neutral sites for the first two rounds, and allow the conference runner-ups to go to the traditional bowl match ups. How would the teams be placed in the bracket? Prior to the start of the college football season a lottery would determine the placement of each conference on the championship bracket (eleven balls in a lottery machine randomly drawn one at a time then placed in one of the starting eleven spots). After all conference champions have been determined, the teams are plugged into the brackets based on their conference and play begins with one round of play each week for a total of four weeks of play. Why not expand this to sixteen teams? Simply too much controversy on who was added and who was left out, conference champions only get to play for a chance at a national title. This eliminates the controversy of power conferences (Big 10, Pac 10, Big 12, etc.) getting the spotlight versus the mid majors (MAC, Mountain West, Conference USA, etc.) best being jilted at bowl time. It is time for a true national championship game not a contrived convenience created by the BCS. As certain non-power conference schools have proved year after year they can play with anybody and beat them. You would think by now the NCAA has learned their lesson with all the revenue created by the NCAA Basketball tourney and apply that logic to football. D1-A football is the only major sport national title not determined by a playoff or sport appropriate system. It is time to get it correct NCAA, not time to create more controversy.

A great source of irony as our Soldiers, Sailors, Airmen, and Marines fight for the freedom of others along with our own freedoms, one of the freedoms upheld this year by the Supreme Court was the first Amendment. The

Westboro Baptist Church that protests at the funerals of service personnel killed in combat or die as a result of said combat are allowed to protest at those funerals. Even though the spirit of the Amendment is being abused, the letter of the law is not; sad but true.

The Fractured Fairy Tale-The American Dream

I was born in the 1960's into a working middle class family.

I was raised in the 1970's by a stay at home mom and a father who was home after work, who was involved in my life.

- I grew up in a small town in western Illinois; a farming community, were hard work was prized. Success came by your own two hands, not on the back of someone else's labor and definitely not handed to you.
- Your neighbors helped your parents keep an eye on you and if you found trouble, there was no denying your part in it.
- Scouts, church, and the school were the guides to an upright and ethical life.
- Manners were expected and not to be forgotten. Common courtesy meant something, not to be practiced only when you felt like it but practiced all the time.
- When there was a difficult time, a death in the household or other tragedy, your neighbors helped, they were not afraid to lend a hand, or bring over food to feed you and yours.

I came of age in the 1980's, into a time when the selflessness of a generation, the baby boomers, brought greed and excess to the forefront.

- The rise of two income families and the coining of the term "latch key kids."
- The beginning of the breakdown of the idea of community, the beginning of when the phrase "fences make good neighbors."

- The beginning of the decline of our civilization, where manners and common courtesies were only reserved for friends and family and not extended to strangers, no way, no how, never to anyone you did not know.
- The rise of the Yuppie, where in the elitist neighborhood you had to keep pace with your neighbors and failure to do so was an unconscionable act. The rise of Suburbatory, cookie cutter houses, cookie cutter people with cookie cutter cubical jobs. Entire suburban areas that are essentially a boring bologna, processed cheese, and mayo sandwiches on white bread served with a side of blandness.
- In this time, I went away to college for the first time. Interesting enough it would have cost less for me to attend the University of Iowa instead of the University of Illinois, a two thousand dollar difference even paying out of state tuition. I did not choose either but a smaller in state public university at about one-sixth the cost of the University of Illinois.

  I became a parent in the 1990's.
- Under educated and working with the skills I had acquired I was barely able to provide the necessities.
- In the decade of the 1990's we saw the rise of being "politically correct." The sanitizing of our society where speaking out and calling something what it was; for example, a lazy, unmotivated, and unemployed individual is not "economically challenged" and does not deserve to be coddled by society.
- We began to see the second and sometimes the third generation of welfare recipients continuing to perpetuate the "helplessness" and abuse the system.

- We see the gap begin to widen between those who have the wealth and those who are the working poor, the slow eroding of the middle class, and the booming cost of higher education.

    At the turn of the twenty-first century, I was back in school, completing my education.

- I was beginning to see the light at the end of the tunnel. I was beginning to live the American dream of job security, family, middle class life style, and financial security.
- This was the decade of the eroding of our freedoms. An act of terror frightened us to the point that our government in the excuse of protecting us from outside threats began to attack our civil liberties.
- We, as a nation, became embroiled in wars in two sovereign nations with no clear options for victory or for withdrawal.
- I salute every soldier, sailor, marine, airman, and private citizen who has given all of themselves so others may be free of tyranny and so we, the common citizen, can go to sleep every night without fear and know someone out there is giving their all for our safety. We, as a nation, must honor these men and women when they return to our shores and we cannot forget those who returned in caskets or not at all.
- As the decade ended, we saw the collapse of our economy, a collapse fuel by greed and excess.

    Now as the decade turns again we are in the midst of an economic downturn.

- The problem in a nutshell is this: Inequality in this country has hit a level that has been seen only once in the nation's history and unemployment has reached a level that has been seen only once since the Great Depression, and at the same time, corporate profits are at a record high. In other words, in the never-ending tug-of-war between "labor" and "capital," there has rarely, if ever, been a time when "capital" was so clearly winning.

- Citizens are protesting in the streets across our nation.
- If America cannot figure out a way to address the issues, the country will likely become increasingly "destabilized," as sociologists might say, and in that scenario, the current protests will likely be only the beginning.
- Let us start with the obvious: Unemployment. Three years after the financial crisis, the unemployment rate is still at the highest level since the Great Depression (except for a brief blip in the early 1980s).
- It is not that unemployment these days is a quick, painful jolt, a record percentage of unemployed people have been unemployed for longer than 6 months. It is not just construction workers who cannot find jobs, the median duration of all unemployment is also near an all-time high.
- Corporate profits as a percent of the economy are near a record all-time high. With the exception of a brief happy period in 2007 (just before the crash), profits are higher than they have been since the 1950s. They are vastly higher than they have been for most of the intervening half-century.
- The average CEO pay is now 350X the average worker's, up from 50X from 1960-1985.

- CEO pay has skyrocketed 300% since 1990. Corporate profits have doubled. Average "production worker" pay has increased 4%.
- While CEOs and shareholders have been cashing in, wages as a percent of the economy have dropped to an all-time low.
- Of course, life is great if you are in the top 1% of American wage earners. You are hauling in a bigger percentage of the country's total pre-tax income than you have at any time since the late 1920s. Your share of the national income, in fact, is almost two times the long-term average. In fact, income inequality has gotten so extreme here that the US now ranks 93rd (this is not a good metric by comparison Sweden's top 1% earns 23 times the income of an average worker while in US the top 1% on average earn 45 times the income of an average worker) in the world in "income equality." China is ahead of us. So is India. So is Iran.
- By the way, few people would have a problem with inequality if the American Dream were still intact, if it were easy to work your way into that top 1%. However, unfortunately, social mobility in this country is also near an all-time low.
- So what does all this mean in terms of net worth? Well, for starters, it means that the top 1% of Americans own 42% of the financial wealth in this country. The top 5%, meanwhile, own nearly 70%.
- HENRY's (High Earners, Not Rich Yet), most of whom are doctors, lawyers, and other professionals with loads of education related debt are suffering along with the

average laborer. Think of this, nearly seventy-five percent of the work force earns below $50,000 a year.

- Remember that huge debt problem we have, with hundreds of millions of Americans indebted up to their eyeballs? Well, the top 1% does not have that problem; they only own 5% of the country's debt.

As I am a parent of grown children, a grandparent, and once again a parent to be, I fear that the American Dream will be no more than a fairy tale for the next generation with the exception of the top tier of society. The American dream will be for most only seen in the movies or on television, for the 99% of us we will become much like Robert DeNiro's character in *THX 182*, a parody of modern man.

We are nearing the tipping point of a crisis, a civil war between ideologies, between those who hold the wealth and political power and those struggling to make ends meet, between worker and corporation, between the government and the people. I do not advocate armed conflict; frankly, I would like to see it avoided. I would like to see change come through open dialogue and compromise between all parties involved but the pessimist in me thinks that will not happen without some physical conflict along the way. The optimist in me hopes we as a nation can come to an understanding and right our ship. The realist in me knows neither may happen or both may come to fruition, but either way we as a nation are in for a long and possibly rocky road ahead.

Occupy

I cannot always be down at the OWS protest but I can help, and do my part by providing a warm meal to those who are spending all their time there.

- I am of the 99%.
- Do not call me a hippy or lazy because I am unemployed.
- I have a Masters degree in business but you of the 1% tell me that I should be thankful for a minimum wage job. Net monthly income on minimum wage (if you work 40 hours per week) is approximately $936 after taxes and before any benefits (if offered) are subtracted.
- Average debt carried by college graduates is twenty-five thousand of college related expense, estimated time to pay off these expenses is a minimum of fifteen years.
- About 70% of high school students go on for further education but only about 25% graduate with a bachelors degree. For easy numbers approximately 18 students out of every 100 students who graduate high school also earn a bachelors degree from a college or university.
- Think about this: Nationally 82% of the US workforce is uneducated or undereducated. Approximately 47% of US workers earn under $25k/year and approximately 75% of US workers earn under $50k/year and approximately 6% of US workers earn over $100k/year; average household expenses for a family of four equates to 77% of gross income and average family income is approximately $62k/year so expenses equate to $48k/year.

A short song list that was the just some of the background music while compiling this book and before you asks my music collection is quite eclectic.

- Romeo Void "Never Say Never"
- Metallica from the S&M album "One"
- Stone Sour "Bother"
- Teribus "Gavotten"
- Trans Siberian Orchestra "Mephistopheles"
- The Beatles "Let it Be"
- Black Sabbath "War Pigs"
- Iron Maiden "Tears of the Dragon"
- Flogging Molly "Far Away Boys"
- Dropkick Murphy's "The Warriors Code"
- Wine and Alchemy "Farewell to Eirinn"
- Motorhead "Ace of Spades"
- Nightwish "Nemo"
- Iced Earth "Crown of the fallen"